AMAZING ANIMALS OF THE WORLD 3

Volume 6

Markhor — Peccary, Collared

GROLIER

an imprint of

Scholastic Library Publishing

www.scholastic.com/librarypublishing

First published 2006 by Grolier, an imprint of Scholastic Library Publishing

For information address the publisher: Grolier, Scholastic Library Publishing
90 Old Sherman Turnpike
Danbury, CT 06816

10 digit: Set ISBN: 0-7172-6179–4; Volume ISBN: 0-7172-6185–9
13 digit: Set ISBN: 978-0-7172-6179–6; Volume ISBN: 978-0-7172-6185–7

Printed and bound in the U.S.A.

Library of Congress Cataloging-in-Publications Data:
Amazing animals of the world 3.
p.cm.
Includes indexes.
Contents: v. 1. Abalone, Black–Butterfly, Giant Swallowtail -- v. 2. Butterfly, Indian Leaf–Dormouse, Garden -- v. 3. Duck, Ferruginous–Glassfish, Indian -- v. 4. Glider, Sugar–Isopod, Freshwater -- v. 5. Jackal, Side-Striped–Margay -- v. 6. Markhor–Peccary, Collared -- v. 7. Pelican, Brown–Salamander, Spotted -- v. 8. Salamander, Two Lined–Spider, Barrel -- v. 9. Spider, Common House–Tuna, Albacore -- v. 10. Tunicate, Light-Bulb–Zebra, Grevy's.
ISBN 0–7172–6179–4 (set : alk. paper) -- ISBN 0–7172–6180–8 (v. 1 : alk. paper) -- ISBN 0-7172-6181–6 (v. 2 : alk. paper) -- ISBN 0-7172-6182–4 (v. 3 : alk. paper) -- ISBN 0-7172-6183–2 (v. 4 : alk. paper) -- ISBN 0-7172-6184–0 (v. 5 : alk. paper) -- ISBN 0-7172-6185–9 (v. 6 : alk. paper) -- ISBN 0-7172-6186–7 (v. 7 : alk. paper) -- ISBN 0-7172-6187–5 (v. 8 : alk. paper) -- ISBN 0-7172-6188–3 (v. 9 : alk. paper) -- ISBN 0-7172-6189–1 (v. 10 : alk.paper)
1. Animals--Juvenile literature. I. Grolier (Firm) II. Title: Amazing animals of the world three.
QL49.A455 2006
590—dc22
2006010870

About This Set

Amazing Animals of the World 3 brings you pictures of 400 exciting creatures, and important information about how and where they live.

Each page shows just one species, or individual type, of animal. They all fall into seven main categories, or groups, of animals (classes and phylums scientifically) identified on each page with an icon (picture)—amphibians, arthropods, birds, fish, mammals, other invertebrates, and reptiles. Short explanations of what these group names mean, and other terms used commonly in the set, appear on page 4 in the Glossary.

Scientists use all kinds of groupings to help them sort out the types of animals that exist today and once wandered the earth (extinct species). *Kingdoms*, *classes*, *phylums*, *genus*, and *species* are among the key words here that are also explained in the Glossary.

Where animals live is important to know as well. Each of the species in this set lives in a particular place in the world, which you can see outlined on the map on each page. And in those places, the animals tend to favor a particular habitat—an environment the animal finds suitable for life—with food, shelter, and safety from predators that might eat it. There they also find ways to coexist with other animals in the area that might eat somewhat different food, use different homes, and so on.

Each of the main habitats is named on the page and given an icon, or picture, to help you envision it. The habitat names are further defined in the Glossary on page 4.

As well as being part of groups like species, animals fall into other categories that help us understand their lives or behavior. You will find these categories in the Glossary on page 4, where you will learn about carnivores, herbivores, and other types of animals.

And there is more information you might want about an animal—its size, diet, where it lives, and how it carries on its species—the way it creates its young. All these facts and more appear in the data boxes at the top of each page.

Finally, the set is arranged alphabetically by the most common name of the species. That puts most beetles, for example, together in a group so you can compare them easily.

But some animals' names are not so common, and they don't appear near others like them. For instance, the chamois is a kind of goat or antelope. To find animals that are similar—or to locate any species—look in the Index at the end of each book in the set (pages 45–48). It lists all animals by their various names (you will find the Giant South American River Turtle under Turtle, Giant South American River, and also under its other name— Arrau). And you will find all birds, fish, and so on gathered under their broader groupings.

Similarly, smaller like groups appear in the Set Index as well—butterflies include swallowtails and blues, for example.

Table of Contents
Volume 6

Glossary

Amphibians—species usually born from eggs in water or wet places, which change (metamorphose) into land animals. Frogs and salamanders are typical. They breathe through their skin mainly and have no scales.

Arctic and Antarctic—icy, cold, dry areas at the ends of the globe that lack trees but see small plants grown in thawed areas (tundra). Penguins and seals are common inhabitants.

Arthropods—animals with segmented bodies, hard outer skin, and jointed legs, such as spiders and crabs.

Birds—born from eggs, these creatures have wings and often can fly. Eagles, pigeons, and penguins are all birds, though penguins cannot fly through the air.

Carnivores—they are animals that eat other animals. Many species do eat each other sometimes, and a few eat dead animals. Lions kill their prey and eat it, while vultures clean up dead bodies of animals.

Cities, Towns, and Farms—places where people live and have built or used the land and share it with many species. Sometimes these animals live in human homes or just nearby.

Class—part or division of a phylum.

Deserts—dry, often warm areas where animals often are more active on cooler nights or near water sources. Owls, scorpions, and jack rabbits are common in American deserts.

Endangered—some animals in this set are marked as endangered because it is possible they will become extinct soon.

Extinct—these species have died out altogether for whatever reason.

Family—part of an order.

Fish—water animals (aquatic) that typically are born from eggs and breathe through gills. Trout and eels are fish, though whales and dolphins are not (they are mammals).

Forests and Mountains—places where evergreen (coniferous) and leaf-shedding (deciduous) trees are common, or that rise in elevation to make cool, separate habitats. Rain forests are different. (see Rain forests)

Fresh Water—lakes, rivers, and the like carry fresh water (unlike Oceans and Shores, where the water is salty). Fish and birds abound, as do insects, frogs, and mammals.

Genus—part of a family.

Grasslands—habitats with few trees and light rainfall. Grasslands often lie between forests and deserts, and they are home to birds, coyotes, antelope, and snakes, as well as many other kinds of animals.

Herbivores—these animals eat mainly plants. Typically they are hoofed animals (ungulates) that are common on grasslands, such as antelope or deer. Domestic (nonwild) ones are cows and horses.

Hibernators—species that live in harsh areas with very cold winters slow down their functions then and sort of sleep through the hard times.

Invertebrates—animals that lack backbones or internal skeletons. Many, such as insects and shrimp, have hard outer coverings. Clams and worms are also invertebrates.

Kingdom—the largest division of species. Commonly there are understood to be five kingdoms: animals, plants, fungi, protists, and monerans.

Mammals—these creatures usually bear live young and feed them on milk from the mother. A few lay eggs (monotremes like the platypus) or nurse young in a pouch (marsupials like opossums and kangaroos).

Migrators—some species spend different seasons in different places, moving to where more food, warmth, or safety can be found. Birds often do this, sometimes over long distances, but other types of animals also move seasonally, including fish and mammals.

Oceans and Shores—seawater is salty, often deep, and huge. In it live many fish, invertebrates, and even some mammals, such as whales. On the shore, birds and other creatures often gather.

Order—part of a class.

Phylum—part of a kingdom.

Rain forests—here huge trees grow among many other plants helped by the warm, wet environment. Thousands of species of animals also live in these rich habitats.

Reptiles—these species have scales, lungs to breathe, and lay eggs or give birth to live young. Dinosaurs are thought to have been reptiles, while today the class includes turtles, snakes, lizards, and crocodiles.

Scientific name—the genus and species name of a creature in Latin. For instance, Canis lupus is the wolf. Scientific names avoid the confusion possible with common names in any one language or across languages.

Species—a group of the same type of living thing. Part of an order.

Subspecies—a variant but quite similar part of a species.

Territorial—many animals mark out and defend a patch of ground as their home area. Birds and mammals may call quite small or quite large spots their territories.

Vertebrates—animals with backbones and skeletons under their skins

Markhor
Capra falconeri

Length: 4½ to 6 feet
Weight: 70 to 240 pounds
Diet: grasses and other plant matter
Number of Young: 1 or 2

Home: Central Asia
Order: Even-toed hoofed mammals
Family: Bovines

 Forests and Mountains

 Mammals

? Endangered Animals

© DAVID C. FRITTS / ANIMALS ANIMALS / EARTH SCENES

The markhor is a wild goat whose name comes from Persian words meaning "snake horn," a perfect description of the snakelike twisting shape of their impressive horns. The horns of a male markhor may be more than 5 feet long when measured along the spiral. Females are smaller than males and have much shorter horns. The male markhor has a long mane of hair on its back and a fluffy beard. Females lack a long mane, and their beard is thin.

Markhor live on high, steep mountains in Central Asia. In summer, they can be found at elevations of up to 12,000 feet. They move to lower places for the winter. These animals are superb climbers and are able to move quickly along rough, rocky ground. Markhor rest in the middle of the day. They graze in the early morning and in the evening. Often they will stand on their back legs to feed on trees and bushes, and may even climb into a tree to reach leaves.

During most of the year, markhor live in small groups. Some groups consist of females and their young. Other groups consist of males. In the breeding season, these groups join to form larger herds.

The enemies of markhor include leopards, wolves, and lynx. But their worst enemies are people who kill these majestic animals for their beautiful horns. As a result, markhor are in danger of becoming extinct.

Pygmy Marmoset
Cebuella pygmaea

Length: 7 to 7½ inches
Length of the Tail: 7½ inches
Weight: 4 to 6½ ounces
Diet: insects, spiders, lizards, fruits, tree gum, and sap

Number of Young: 2 (twins)
Home: South America
Order: Primates
Family: Marmosets and tamarins

 Rain forests

 Mammals

The pygmy marmoset is the smallest monkey in the world. Although it is abundant in the rain forests of the upper Amazon, it is very difficult to spot. This clever creature is an expert at concealing itself from the many dangerous predators to be found in its habitat. When danger is near, it can freeze as still as a statue. Then, when the coast is clear, it quickly springs from one branch to another.

The pygmy marmoset spends most of its time feasting on its favorite snack: the nutritious sap and gum that oozes from different types of tropical trees. To get more of this treat, the marmoset gnaws a hole in the tree bark with its lower front teeth. It may bore hundreds of these holes into a single tree. When it is not sap-sucking, the pygmy marmoset also eats an occasional spider or small lizard, or dines on a juicy piece of fruit.

Pygmy marmosets are nurturing parents. But unlike most mammals, it is the father, not the mother, who cares for the newborns. He helps the mother deliver the bean-sized babies, which are usually twins. He then feeds them and cares for them, while mother guards the tree house. Father also takes the twins out for walks, carrying them around his neck, where they cling like tiny scarves. Pygmy marmosets mate for life.

House Martin
Delichon urbica

Length: about 5 inches
Wingspan: 10 to 11 inches
Weight: about ½ ounce
Diet: insects
Number of Eggs: 2 to 6

Home: Europe, Africa, and Asia
Order: Perching birds
Family: True swallows

 Cities, Towns, and Farms

 Birds

© STEPHEN DALTON / NHPA

Like other swallows, the house martin has a forked tail; a short, gaping bill; and long, pointed wings. To distinguish it from other European swallows, look for its pure-white rump. This species usually flies higher than other swallows and prefers to flutter, rather than swoop, when catching its prey.

As its name implies, the house martin often plasters its mud nest under the eaves of houses and barns. House martins are so comfortable around humans that they even breed in big cities such as London. They will boldly gather mud within several feet of human observers. Away from civilization, house martins nest on sea cliffs and the rock faces of mountains.

Wherever they nest, house martins crowd together, their mud nests often touching.

These birds also join in large groups when they migrate in the fall. Flocks of more than 400 birds have been seen on their way to tropical Africa. If the flock is caught in bad weather while traveling, the martins may stop and cling to the sides of a house until the storm passes.

House martins feed almost entirely on flying insects such as aphids and flies, although they occasionally peck insects off the ground and walls. Typically a martin catches its prey in flight while keeping its mouth wide open. House martins have even been known to fly behind tractors gulping down the insects that are churned into the air.

7

Common Mayfly
Ephemera vulgata

Length of the Body: ½ to ⅞ inch
Length of the Tail: ⅞ to 1⅜ inches
Diet: decaying leaves and microorganisms

Number of Eggs: 5,000
Home: Europe
Order: Mayflies
Family: Burrowing mayflies

 Fresh Water

 Arthropods

© HANS PFLETSCHINGER / PETER ARNOLD, INC.

The mayfly can be found buzzing over clear, slow-moving streams throughout Europe during the month of—you guessed it—May. In some places, mayflies can also be seen in June, July, or August.

Whenever and wherever they are found, mayflies appear for only a short time. They live for two years. But they spend most of their lives underwater in an immature form. The winged adult lives for only two or three days—just long enough to find a mate, lay eggs, and die. Adult mayflies live such a short time that they never even eat!

Amazingly, all the adult mayflies in a stream emerge from the water at the same time. The males form huge swarms. To attract females, the male swarm zooms straight up several yards above the water and then slowly drifts back down. After mating, the females deposit their eggs on the surface of the water. The eggs immediately sink and hatch 10 or 11 days later. The young, wingless mayflies—called naiads—burrow into the mud and build underground nests.

The naiad outgrows its skin several times, always growing a new, larger one. Just before it emerges from the water, it sheds a skin to reveal a new winged body. It then swims to the surface and flies to a nearby rock to dry off. After 24 to 30 hours, it sheds its skin one last time and emerges ready to mate. The mayfly is the only insect in the world that sheds its skin after it grows wings.

Feather Midge
Chironomus plumosus

Length: about 1/10 inch
Diet: dead plant and animal matter and other dissolved nutrients (larva)
Method of Reproduction: egg layer

Home: North America, Europe, and northern Africa
Order: Mosquitoes, flies, and their relatives
Family: Nonbiting midges

 Fresh Water

 Arthropods

© KIM TAYLOR / BRUCE COLEMAN INC.

The feather midge is a harmless insect named for the male's feathery antennae. The creature's long legs are also covered with small hairs. At rest the feather midge often sits back on its hind legs, while stretching its frilly front legs high in the air. Feather midges are most abundant near ponds and streams. At night, they often swarm around lit windows and streetlights.

Feather midges are very common insects that resemble mosquitoes both in appearance and in their habit of swarming. Fortunately for humans and other mammals, feather midges do not bite. They are actually quite beneficial; they constitute an abundant source of food for fish and birds.

Feather midges mate in swarms in and around water. The females deposit their eggs on the surface and on aquatic plants. The eggs hatch into immature larvae that contain a red pigment. This pigment is almost identical to a substance called hemoglobin, which is found in human blood. Like hemoglobin, the midge larva's red pigment is able to absorb oxygen. So the pigment enables the larvae to extract oxygen even in the most oxygen-poor water. This allows feather midges to survive in stagnant and polluted ponds and lakes. In fact, scientists sometimes call oxygen-poor lakes "plumosis lakes," referring to this midge's scientific name.

Red-Tailed Shark Minnow
Labeo bicolor

Length: up to 5 inches
Diet: algae, small insects, and crustaceans
Method of Reproduction: egg layer

Home: Thailand
Order: Carps and their relatives
Family: Minnows

 Fresh Water

 Fish

© BILL HOWES / FRANK LANE PICTURE AGENCY / CORBIS

The red-tailed shark is actually a tropical minnow, named for the shape of its sharklike body and dorsal fin. Its appetite, however, could not be more unsharklike. Red-tailed sharks can survive by scraping algae off rocks with their sucker-shaped mouths. They occasionally supplement their vegetarian diet with a meal of brine shrimp.

Its dramatic coloring makes the red-tailed shark a popular freshwater aquarium pet. A black body and bright red tail stand out in any crowd. But do not be tempted to fill your aquarium with these feisty fish. As a rule, red-tailed sharks do not get along with each other and will fight fiercely if kept in close quarters. Fortunately, they coexist fairly peaceably with other species.

Red-tailed sharks breed well in captivity. As a result, those sold in pet stores no longer come from the wild. This is good news for conservationists, who warn that too many tropical fish are being collected from natural populations.

When she is ready to mate, the female red-tailed shark scatters her eggs across the bottom of her tank (or the bottom of a streambed if she lives in the wild). The male follows close behind to fertilize the eggs. Unlike many freshwater fish, which guard their eggs and young, red-tailed sharks simply swim away and let the young fish fend for themselves.

Indian Gray Mongoose
Herpestes edwardsi

Length of the Body: up to 17 inches
Length of the Tail: up to 16 inches
Diet: small mammals, birds, reptiles, carcasses, and fruits

Weight: up to 3 pounds
Number of Young: 2 to 4
Home: southern Asia
Order: Carnivores
Family: Viverrids, aardwolves, and hyenas

 Cities, Towns, and Farms

 Mammals

© DANIEL HEUCLIN / NHPA / PHOTO RESEARCHERS

Within the family of animals known as viverrids, there are 30 species of mongoose. All are slender predators with a lean body, short limbs, and long, wiry fur. Like other viverrids, mongooses have a small head with a pointed snout and sharp teeth.

The Indian gray mongoose is one of the most familiar in its family. This medium-size viverrid is famous the world over as a snake killer. Its battles with cobras are legendary. How does the mongoose survive an encounter with such a deadly snake? First the mongoose is very quick, so it can jump and twist its body, trying to avoid the cobra's strike. Also, it is partly immune to the snake's venom. With much dodging and leaping, the mongoose is usually able to kill the cobra with a quick, yet powerful, bite to its neck.

In addition to catching snakes, the Indian gray mongoose kills rats and other rodent pests. The species would be more valued by humans if it did not attack chickens and other small domestic animals. Still, many villagers tame young mongooses and keep them near their homes to control the population of rodents and snakes.

The mongoose is most active during the day and often lives in towns and farms. Although it is a skillful predator, it scavenges through garbage and steals fruit from orchards. These mongooses usually avoid each other outside of breeding season.

Common Monitor (Water Monitor)
Varanus salvator

Length: up to 8 feet
Diet: small to medium-size animals
Number of Eggs: up to 60

Home: Indonesia
Order: Lizards and snakes
Family: Monitor lizards

 Rain forests

 Reptiles

© MARIAN BACON / ANIMALS ANIMALS / EARTH SCENES

At 8 feet the common, or water, monitor rivals the great Komodo dragon (*Varanus komodoensis*) in length. But the massive Komodo weighs several times more than this close cousin. Two-thirds of the common monitor's length is made up of tail. The tail is flattened from side to side, enabling it to perform as a powerful propeller in water. When swimming, the monitor lashes its tail with sideways strokes.

In addition to being a powerful swimmer, the common monitor lizard is a swift climber. Moving slowly up tree trunks and across large branches, it hunts for sleeping birds and other small- to medium-size animals. Common monitors are strictly meat eaters. They get the extra "plant" vitamins they need by licking out the stomachs of herbivorous (plant-eating) prey. This lizard is an important predator on the jungle islands of Indonesia. A fully grown common monitor has no wild enemies, although young monitor lizards are sometimes eaten by large snakes. Humans kill monitors for their valuable skins, which are stuffed and sold as souvenirs in tourist shops.

The males of this species are territorial and aggressive toward one another. But their shoving matches seldom result in serious harm. Generally two males face off by rearing up on their hind legs and pushing. They rarely bite, and the weaker of the two eventually withdraws.

Humboldt's Woolly Monkey
Lagothrix lagotricha

Length: 16 to 23 inches (without tail); up to 4 feet with tail
Weight: 12 to 15 pounds
Diet: fruit, insects, small animals, leaves, and flowers

Number of Young: 1
Home: Amazon basin of South America
Order: Primates
Family: New World monkeys

 Forests and Mountains

 Mammals

© ART WOLFE / PHOTO RESEARCHERS

? Endangered Animals

The woolly monkey is one of the largest of all South American monkeys. It has a very long tail that can curl tightly around branches. This monkey lives in trees, where it moves about by hanging by its arms. After a trip through the trees, it sometimes rests dangling from a branch by its tail. It can walk on four legs or upright, using its arms for balance.

Woolly monkeys live in groups of 15 to 40. Their territory can stretch over 4 square miles. They cover about half a mile a day searching for food—fruit, tender leaves, small animals, flowers, and insects. They live in palm forests that are near rivers and on the wooded slopes of the Andes Mountains. At night, they sleep stretched out on a branch, arms and legs bent and tails curled around their bodies.

The Humboldt's woolly monkey is an endangered species; this is due to many factors. It reproduces slowly, only once every 1½ to 2 years. The female gives birth to a single baby after a pregnancy of over seven months. The baby nurses for at least one year, and it will not be old enough to reproduce until it is four or five. South American Indians hunt the woolly monkeys for their meat, and they are often captured as pets. But the most serious danger to the woolly monkey is the destruction of the forests where it lives: its home territory is getting smaller and smaller each year.

Moorish Idol (Kihikihi)
Zanclus canescens

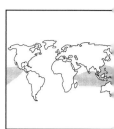

Length: up to 7 inches
Diet: algae and marine invertebrates
Method of Reproduction: egg layer

Home: Indian Ocean and central Pacific Ocean
Order: Perchlike fishes
Family: Surgeonfishes

 Oceans and Shores

 Fish

© ROBERT YIN / CORBIS

Legend has it that the Moorish people regarded this gorgeous fish with great respect. If accidentally captured, it was returned to the water with great care and a ceremonial bow—a ritual for which the Moorish idol gained its common name. Like the Moors, native Hawaiians also know and appreciate this fish. But unlike the Moors, they call it kihikihi and eat the fish's tasty meat with great relish!

The adult Moorish idol has a long, flowing fin that extends from a spine on its back. This ribbonlike extension, along with two horny bumps in front of the eyes, gets larger as the fish ages. As a result, young and old Moorish idols look quite different from each other. In the 1700s, scientists named the younger fish "gray chaetodon."

Thinking that the adult was a different species, they called it the "horned chaetodon." Young Moorish idols have yet another distinction: a knifelike spine behind each corner of its mouth. These sharp spines drop off when the fish reaches about 3 inches in length.

Moorish idols are common near the tropical coral reefs of the Pacific and Indian oceans. They seldom swim deeper than 5 feet as they graze among the reef's nooks and crannies. These fish swim in pairs or small schools and occasionally mix with groups of butterflyfish and angelfish. Little is known about the Moorish idol's mating habits. Like its close relatives, it probably mates at dusk on the slope of a coral reef.

Malaria Mosquito
Anopheles spp.

Length: ¼ to ⅓ of an inch
Wingspan: up to ⅓ of an inch
Diet: nectar, fruit juices, and blood
Method of Reproduction: egg layer

Home: worldwide
Order: Flies and mosquitoes
Family: Mosquitoes
Subfamily: Malaria mosquitoes

Fresh Water

Arthropods

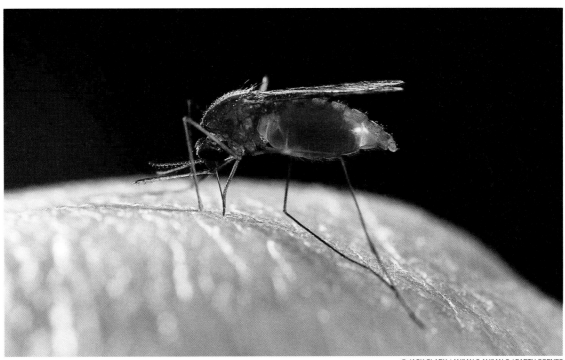

© JACK CLARK / ANIMALS ANIMALS / EARTH SCENES

Malaria mosquitoes live nearly anywhere there is stagnant water: swamps, rice fields, irrigation ditches, and mud puddles. This mosquito carries the organism that causes malaria in humans. The one-celled organism breeds inside the female mosquito. She can then pass it on to whomever she bites. The infected person can also pass malaria to still more mosquitoes when they draw blood. And so the cycle continues.

Health workers have found that the best way to control malaria is to stop malaria mosquitoes from breeding. Usually this means altering the environment by draining swamps, keeping ditches dry, and pouring oil on standing water. This deprives the female mosquito of a wet place for her eggs. If she can find open water, the female mosquito drops her eggs singly across the surface. Each egg comes equipped with a tiny, air-filled float. After a few days, the floating eggs hatch into legless larvae, called "wrigglers," that lie just below the water's surface. The larvae change shape several times before maturing into adults and swarming from the water.

Adult malaria mosquitoes can be recognized by their long, slender legs and striped wings. Both sexes feed on nectar and fruit juices. The female must take blood in order to produce her eggs. She finds a human host by using both her sight and her sense of smell.

Imperial Moth
Eacles imperialis

Wingspan: 4 to 6 inches
Method of Reproduction: egg layer
Home: eastern United States; Ontario and Quebec

Diet: adults do not feed
Order: Butterflies and moths
Family: Giant silkworm moths and royal moths

 Forests and Mountains

 Arthropods

© FRED WHITEHEAD / ANIMALS ANIMALS / EARTH SCENES

The dramatic imperial moth may be declining in areas where there are many artificial lights. Like most moths, this nocturnal species is attracted to lamps, where it is easily spotted by nighttime predators such as insect-eating bats. Imperial moths also have the habit of flitting near outdoor lights until dawn. With the daylight comes danger, and many imperial moths are eaten by birds and other early risers.

In the northern part of its range, the adult imperial moth emerges from the ground in late spring. Without ever bothering to eat, it mates, lays eggs, and dies. From the eggs hatch large, fleshy caterpillars, covered with yellow, bristly bumps. Imperial caterpillars grow to nearly 6 inches as they feed on the leaves of many different trees, including birch, elm, maple, oak, walnut, and cedar.

In the southern part of its range, where the warm season is longer, the imperial moth produces two generations each year. The caterpillars born in spring have time to turn into moths by midsummer. This second generation of moths lays eggs that hatch in August or September. When they have finished feeding, the fall caterpillars dig into the ground. They wrap themselves in a kind of cocoon and overwinter in special underground cells. There the caterpillars transform into adult moths, which emerge the following spring.

Oak Eggar Moth
Lasiocampa quercus

Wingspan: 2½ to 3½ inches
Diet of the Caterpillar: leaves and plant parts
Method of Reproduction: egg layer

Home: Eurasia and northern Africa
Order: Butterflies and moths
Family: Lasiocampids

 Forests and Mountains

 Arthropods

© DUNCAN MCEWAN / NATURE PICTURE LIBRARY

During the day the male oak eggar moth flies through the forest in search of females that may be resting on branches and tree trunks. He usually finds and breeds with several each day. At night the mated females fly over small trees and shrubs, dropping their eggs as they go. These moths do not eat; they live only to breed, and then they die.

It is easy to distinguish the male oak eggar from the female. The male's wings, a dark reddish brown with a yellow-orange band, are highlighted by a bright white spot on the front. The female is larger than her mate and has paler wings. She also sports white wing spots, but they are ringed in a dark reddish-brown. The newborn oak eggar caterpillar, or larva, is black with long white hairs and orange bands of color. As the caterpillar matures, it turns brownish-gray with a thick covering of reddish-brown hair.

The caterpillar is a nighttime feeder with a huge appetite for the leaves of hawthorn, bramble, sallow, and blackthorn shrubs. During the day, it crawls off the leaves and moves onto stalks of the shrub. If disturbed, the caterpillar rolls into a ball as if playing dead. Oak eggar caterpillars hibernate through the winter. In spring, they emerge to feed again and spin their cocoons. The name "eggar" comes from the insect's hard egg-shaped cocoon.

Peppered Moth
Biston betularia

Wingspan: 1½ inches
Diet: leaves of deciduous trees
Method of Reproduction: egg
   layer

Home: Eurasia and
   northeastern North America
Order: Butterflies and moths
Family: Geometrid moths

Cities, Towns,
and Farms

Arthropods

© MARTIN B. WITHERS / FRANK LANE PICTURE AGENCY / CORBIS

The peppered moth flaps its wings quite gently and does not fly very far at one time. It is often seen delicately flitting from leaf to leaf in the parks, gardens, and tree-lined avenues of Europe and Asia. As its name suggests, this moth is "peppered" with tiny black spots. However, its coloring varies throughout its range. In some places the peppered moth is nearly white, with just a few spots. In others, it is almost pitch black.

The peppered moth's spots are its camouflage. Just a few spots are enough to help the moth blend in with speckled tree trunks. But in some big cities, the soot from factories and fireplaces blackens the tree trunks, as well as poles, buildings, and other

perching sites. In these places, darkly spotted moths have a better chance of hiding from hungry birds and other enemies. As a result the more soot there is in a city, the more darkly spotted the peppered moths are in the area.

Like all moths and butterflies, this species begins life as a caterpillar. The peppered-moth caterpillar moves like an inchworm. With each step, it creates a little loop in the middle of its body, with its tail and head almost touching. When bothered, peppered moth caterpillars lift up their front end so as to resemble a small twig. Sometimes this disguise fools a predator, which then moves on in search of another victim.

Silkworm Moth
Bombyx mori

Length of Larva: 3 to 3½ inches
Wingspan of Adult: about 1¾ inches
Diet: mulberry leaves

Number of Eggs: up to 700
Home: native to China; introduced elsewhere
Order: Butterflies and moths
Family: Silkworms

 Cities, Towns, and Farms

 Arthropods

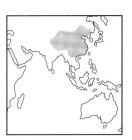

© HANS PFLETSCHINGER / PETER ARNOLD, INC.

The silkworm moth is a small white moth with a pair of large antennae on its head. People raise the silkworm moth for the silk it produces when it is in the caterpillar stage. At birth the caterpillars are only ½ inch long. They are fed leaves from certain kinds of mulberry trees. By the time the caterpillars are five weeks old, they are about 3 inches long and fully grown.

The silkworm-moth caterpillar spins a cocoon of silk thread around itself and enters the pupa stage. Left alone, the insect will metamorphose, or change, into an adult moth. People in the silk business collect the cocoons and heat them. This heating kills the insects. Then the cocoons are soaked in hot water to soften the gum that holds together the silk thread. This permits the thread to be unrolled. A cocoon consists of a thread from 3,000 to 5,000 feet long. About 3,000 cocoons are needed to produce one pound of silk.

China is the world's main silk producer. The silkworm moth was domesticated in China almost 5,000 years ago. Around the 4th century A.D., people began to raise silk moths in Japan and India. Later, production began elsewhere. Attempts to cultivate silkworm moths in North America were never successful, partly because of a lack of the right varieties of mulberry trees.

Yellow-Necked Field Mouse
Apodemus flavicollis

Length of the Body: 3½ to 5 inches
Length of the Tail: 4 to 5½ inches
Diet: seeds, fruits, insects, and snails

Weight: ¾ to 1½ ounces
Number of Young: 4 to 7
Home: Europe and Asia
Order: Rodents
Family: True mice

Forests and Mountains

Mammals

© UWE WALZ / CORBIS

The yellow-necked field mouse has many enemies, because it is a convenient, bite-sized morsel. As it scampers through the night, this small rodent must avoid owls swooping from the sky, snakes slithering through the trees, and carnivores prowling the forest floor. Fortunately for the yellow-necked field mouse, it comes equipped with an effective "early-warning system." Its big eyes and large, batlike ears can detect the slightest sign of danger in the dark.

This mouse is named for the pale ring of fur around its throat. However, its yellow "necklace" is often broken or faint. As a result, even scientists have a hard time distinguishing this species from its nearly identical cousin, the European wood mouse.

Sometimes these two species are found in the same regions. When they are, they avoid competition by adopting different lifestyles. Generally the yellow-necked field mouse retreats to the damp and leafy center of the woods. The wood mouse stays in the dry, open meadows. Even when they invade the same house, these two mice often choose different quarters.

Whether in the forest or in someone's house, the yellow-necked field mouse is sure to build a small lodge, or food chamber. This storage room may be in a wall or between some roots or rocks. The mouse usually keeps a separate nest for sleeping, often beneath a fallen tree or high up in a deserted bird's nest.

Indian Muntjac (Barking Deer)
Muntiacus muntjak

Length: 3 to 4½ feet
Weight: 33 to 77 pounds
Number of Young: 1 to 2
Diet: herbs, sprouts, fruits, eggs, small animals, and carrion

Home: India, Indonesia, Java, China, and Taiwan
Order: Even-toed ungulates
Family: Deer, elk, and moose
Subfamily: Muntjac deer
Suborder: Ruminants

 Rain forests

 Mammals

© DAVID HOSKING / FRANK LANE PICTURE AGENCY / CORBIS

This tiny deer is no Bambi! The Indian muntjac is a fearsome hunter that will stomp a small animal to death or bite it fiercely with its pair of long fangs. Muntjacs also raid the nests of ground-dwelling birds and even steal game out of traps set by humans.

Although they sometimes curse the muntjac for stealing their food, Indian hunters seldom take revenge. This deer is an important messenger of danger. Should a tiger or leopard prowl nearby, the muntjac will bark out a loud warning that sounds like the howl of a dog. The noise gives the muntjac its other name, the barking deer.

Muntjacs are not social animals. Each ferociously defends its own small territory, usually a patch of jungle about ¹⁄₁₀th of a square mile. A muntjac will not even tolerate another deer of the opposite sex—except when it is ready to mate. Motherhood does not soften the muntjac's territorial behavior. When her fawns are six months old, a female chases them away from her turf. Young deer that are not strong enough to win a territory of their own may quickly become dinner for a prowling wildcat. The creature's small territory does not contain enough food for everyone. To survive, the deer has learned to fight savagely and eat just about anything—from tree bark to the flesh of dead animals.

Common Murre
Uria aalge

Length: 16 to 17 inches
Diet: fish, crustaceans, mollusks, and worms
Number of Eggs: 1
Size of the Egg: 3 inches

Home: North Pacific and North Atlantic oceans
Order: Water birds
Family: Auks

 Oceans and Shores

 Birds

© CHASE SWIFT / CORBIS

From a distance a colony of common murres looks very much like a rookery of penguins. But instead of a black-and-white tuxedo, the common murre wears a jacket of brown over its white belly. Look closely, and you will also see that the common murre's bill is much narrower than that of a penguin. This bird is the most common member of the auk family, a group of birds that has been called the "penguins of the north." But auks and penguins are only distantly related. They resemble each other because both evolved to live in cold polar seas. Like penguins, auks are built for diving and stand upright on land. Unlike penguins, however, auks such as the murre can still fly.

The common murre spends the entire winter at sea, feeding on fish, crabs, and mollusks, which it catches underwater. When it dives, the murre can hold its breath for more than a minute. Using its powerful wings and webbed feet, it can easily propel itself 100 feet below the surface. When in pursuit of a very tasty-looking fish, the murre has been known to dive as deep as 550 feet.

In spring, murres come ashore to mate. The female lays her single egg on bare rock, usually on a ledge midway up a shoreline cliff. While the eggs of most bird species look alike, murre eggs vary widely in both color and pattern. This may help each mother tell her egg from the many others in the colony.

Bleeding Tooth Mussel
Nerita peloronta

Length: 1½ to 3 inches
Weight: ½ to ¾ ounce
Diet: algae
Home: coastal waters off southeast Florida to Bermuda and the West Indies

Number of Eggs: 300 to 700
Order: Mussels that live on hard surfaces
Family: Mussels with spiral-shaped shells having flattened openings

 Oceans and Shores

Other Invertebrates

© E. R. DEGGINGER / COLOR PIC, INC.

If you have ever strolled along a Caribbean beach, you may remember this unusual mollusk. It looks something like a shellfish vampire, sporting two white "teeth" surrounded by a reddish spot that resembles dried blood. Although this shell is easy to recognize, not even the experts know what the mollusk does with its teethlike projections . . . or why they look bloody.

The bleeding tooth is well adapted to life in warm tropical waters. To stay cool, it avoids direct sunlight by hiding in dark crevices between rocks, stones, and dead coral reefs. The bleeding tooth also attaches itself in the crannies of jetties and the concrete bases of bridges. It anchors itself in place by digging its fleshy foot into a tiny crack. The foot squirts out a sticky substance that cements it in place. So strong is this foot and its glue that not even a crashing wave or a hungry predator can pry the mollusk from its perch.

The bleeding tooth prefers to remain in shallow water, where its favorite food—algae—is most abundant. But life in shallow water is not easy. When the tide flows out, the bleeding-tooth mollusk is left high and dry—sometimes for many hours. To keep from drying out, this mollusk uses a specially designed lid to cover the rim of its shell.

Common Blue Mussel
Mytilus edulis

Length: 1½ to 4 inches
Height: 2 inches
Diet: microscopic organisms
Method of Reproduction: egg
   layer

Home: coasts of Europe and
   North America; introduced
   elsewhere
Order: Mytilids
Family: Marine mussels

 Oceans and
Shores

 Other
Invertebrates

© HANS REINHARD / BRUCE COLEMAN INC.

People in many parts of the world eat the soft, tasty meat of blue mussels. These mussels are very common in coastal waters throughout much of the world. Large clumps of the blue-black shells can be seen attached to rocks, wharf pilings, and other solid objects at the edge of the sea. Each shell consists of two pieces, called valves. The valves are joined at one end by a hinge. This creature opens and closes it shell with a pair of powerful muscles. The shell, which protects the soft body of the animal, is made by a fold of tissue called the mantle, which surrounds the mussel's body. Cells in the mantle remove lime (calcium carbonate) from ocean water and use the lime to construct the shell.

A mussel clings to a rock or other object by means of brownish filaments called byssus threads. The threads are extremely tough, holding the mussel in place even when big waves crash down on it. Usually a mussel stays in one place. But it can break its byssus threads with its muscular foot and slowly creep to a new location, where it reattaches itself with new threads.

A mussel egg hatches into a tiny larva that does not look like an adult mussel. The larva does not have a mantle or shell. Many larvae are eaten or die in the first few weeks, but those that complete maturation begin new lives in the mud of a stream or lake bottom.

Eastern Newt
Notophthalmus viridescens

Length: 1½ to 3¼ inches
Diet: mollusks, insects, and worms
Number of Eggs: 200 to 400

Home: eastern North America
Order: Amphibians with tails
Family: Salamanders
Subfamily: Newts and efts

 Fresh Water

Amphibians

© DAVID T. ROBERTS / NATURE'S IMAGES INC. / PHOTO RESEARCHERS

The eastern newt is a small salamander that lives in the eastern part of North America. It is also known as the red-spotted newt. Like other amphibians, it lives part of its life in water and part on land.

The life of the eastern newt begins in the water. The adult female newt lays her eggs on the leaves of underwater plants in a lake, pond, or stream. The eggs hatch in one to two months. The larvae, or tadpoles, breathe through gills, just like fish. In two or three months, however, they develop lungs. At this point, the young newts make their way onto land. They live on land for up to three years, and during this period of their lives they are known as red efts. The newts then return to the water, where the cycle begins again. During its life cycle, the color of the eastern newt often changes. When it is a tadpole, it is yellowish-green. As it grows, it changes to a bright red, and it has black-bordered red spots on its back. It stays this color when it lives on land. When it returns to the water, its color changes to olive green.

A poison secreted by its skin protects the eastern newt from predators whether it is on land or in the water. If a predator does tear off one of its small legs, it will grow another one. The eastern newt feeds on insects, worms, and mollusks.

Marbled Newt
Triturus marmoratus

Length: 4¾ to 6¼ inches
Diet: worms, insects, larvae, and the eggs of other amphibians and fish
Home: France, Spain, and Portugal

Number of Eggs: 200 to 300
Order: Salamanders and newts
Family: Newts and their relatives

 Forests and Mountains

Amphibians

© CHRIS MATTISON / FRANK LANE PICTURE AGENCY / CORBIS

Male and female marbled newts look quite different. The female can be recognized by the bright orange stripe that runs down the middle of her back. Instead of a stripe, the male has a raised crest extending down his back. The male is also adorned with silvery bands on either side of his tail. Unlike true salamanders, marbled newts are not slimy; their skin is dry and rough.

Marbled newts are rarely seen during the day. They are most active at night, especially after a heavy rain. During most of the year, they live and hunt on land, usually in the woods and heaths near ponds, ditches, and pools of water.

Between February and April, when it is time to breed, the male newt's tail widens into a broad paddle. At the same time, his hind legs enlarge, and black horny bumps appear on the insides of his thighs and toes. During this time, marbled newts leave the woodland floor to gather in the water.

In a typical newt courtship dance, the male swims in front of the female and waves his tail. He then deposits a little ball of sperm, which the female picks up to fertilize her eggs. Although she may lay as many as 300 eggs, the female takes great care to attach them singly to plants in and above the water. The eggs hatch into fishlike larvae that gradually grow legs and lungs.

Palmate Newt
Triturus helveticus

Length: 3 to 3½ inches
Weight: 3 to 5 ounces
Diet: worms, slugs, insects, and crustaceans
Home: England, Scotland, and Central Europe

Number of Eggs: up to 500
Order: Salamanders and newts
Family: Newts and their relatives

 Forests and Mountains

 Amphibians

© MICHAEL MACONACHIE / PAPILIO / CORBIS

The word "palmate" refers to this newt's webbed back feet. Actually, it is only the male of this species that grows webbing between his toes, and only during the mating season. Using his webbed feet like swim fins, the male can move through the water a little faster than a female. When courting a mate, the male palmate newt must swim in front of her to block her path. He then performs an odd courtship dance, wriggling his body and displaying the spots on his skin. As if hypnotized, the female tries to come closer. The male then drops a ball of sperm, which his mate picks up and uses to fertilize her eggs.

Palmate newts spend only half the year in the water. Growing webbed toes is only part of the transformation these newts undergo before leaving dry land. The newt's skin becomes thinner and smoother, enabling it to absorb oxygen from the water directly into its body. Its eyes change shape, so that it can focus clearly underwater. Its tail becomes flattened from side to side, like a long paddle. The palmate newt even develops special organs under its skin that sense vibrations in the water. This enables the newt to detect the movements of underwater prey.

At the end of summer, palmate newts and their young have grown plump from feeding on aquatic insects. Before returning to the forest floor, their skin thickens to prevent their body from losing moisture.

Smooth Newt
Triturus vulgaris

Length: 2¾ to 4½ inches
Diet: larvae, insects, spiders, and earthworms
Home: Europe and western Asia

Number of Eggs: 200 to 400
Order: Salamanders and newts
Family: True newts

Fresh Water

Amphibians

© MARTIN B. WITHERS / FRANK LANE PICTURE AGENCY / CORBIS

On a mild day in late winter or early spring, male smooth newts yearn for water. They crawl out of their hiding places on the forest floor and search for a swamp, lake, or stream. Even a ditch or pond will do, if that is where the newt was born. Once in the water, the male newts quietly wait for the females, who arrive a few days later.

Unlike frogs and toads, who croak and call for their mates, salamanders and newts have little if any voice and only the tiniest of ears. Instead of using song, smooth newts greet their mates with a courtship dance. The male newt leads the female in a simple dance and then deposits a gooey ball of sperm. She picks up the sticky ball and uses it to fertilize her eggs. Then she attaches her eggs to water plants with her back legs.

When they hatch, the young newts look like miniature versions of their parents. The only difference is that newborn newts have gills and breathe water. By the time they are three months old, smooth newts have exchanged their gills for lungs and are ready to crawl out of the water. They will not return until it is their time to mate.

Adult smooth newts travel far from their wet birthplaces into dry woods and meadows. They are more at home on dry land than are any of Europe's other newt species. During the day, smooth newts hunt for grubs and other small creatures beneath fallen leaves and rotting logs.

Eurasian Nightjar
Caprimulgus europaeus

Length: 10 to 11 inches
Diet: moths and other flying insects
Number of Eggs: 2
Egg Size: 1¼ inches

Home: Europe, Africa, and Asia
Order: Goatsuckers, frogmouths, and oilbirds
Family: Nightjars

Forests and Mountains

Birds

☐ Summer
☐ Winter

© ALAN BARNES / NHPA

While other birds fill the day with their flight and song, the Eurasian nightjar sits motionless along a branch or in a bit of dirt. Like a patchwork of dead leaves, the nightjar's mottled brown feathers blend in perfectly with the surroundings. Then, as other birds settle into their roosts at sunset, the nightjar flutters its soft wings and begins its rapid, churring call: "jarr-jarr-jarr." At first the cry of the nightjar might be mistaken for the sound of crickets. But the notes grow longer and louder as the symphony builds to a finale. Then the nightjar silently takes to the air—wheeling and circling, darting and swooping in a crazy, moonlit dance.

The Eurasian nightjar's fanciful flight is not without purpose. The bird is chasing moths and other insects of the night. This small predator has large eyes with keen night vision and a fringe of beak feathers that help it feel for insects in the dark. This fringe also acts like the bristles on a vacuum cleaner, helping to funnel flying insects into the bird's open mouth.

In spring, the nightjar spends much of its time on the ground—choosing a mate and caring for its eggs and young. To woo a female, the male nightjar claps his wings loudly. The couple sway their tails from side to side before mating. The Eurasian nightjar builds no nest. The female simply lays her eggs in a shallow scrape in the dirt. In just 18 days, the eggs hatch, and in another 18 days, the chicks are ready to fly.

Numbat
Myrmecobius fasciatus

Length: 6½ to 10 inches
Diet: almost exclusively termites; some ants
Number of Young: usually 4

Home: southwestern Australia
Order: Marsupials
Family: Marsupial "mice," "moles," and numbats

 Grasslands

 Mammals

© ANN & STEVE TOON / NHPA

 Endangered Animals

At first sight, the numbat, with its bushy tail, may look like a squirrel. But its nose is much thinner, and the black-and-white stripes on its lower back make it impossible to mistake the numbat for any other animal. The numbat is slow, friendly, and defenseless. It lives in eucalyptus forests and bushy savannas. During the day, numbats search the forest for termites, their favorite food. They scratch the ground or dead tree trunks and then quickly pull the insects out with their long, thin, sticky tongues. They swallow the termites whole and can eat from 10,000 to 20,000 a day!

The female numbat raises her young alone. She does not have a pouch to protect her babies as most marsupials do. Instead, the young cling to their mother, who takes them everywhere with her for the first four months. Then she makes a nest in the ground and nurses them for another two months, until they are old enough to live on their own.

Numbats are an endangered species because their environment is being destroyed. Forest fires are killing the insects they eat. Also, people cut down many trees for lumber. These trees were once homes for termites and ants, which the numbat needs for food. Without food to eat, the numbats will die. In addition, foxes, dingoes, and eagles attack numbats. The Australians have created animal reserves to protect numbats, but these reserves have not yet successfully protected the numbat from its enemies.

Eurasian Nutcracker
Nucifraga caryocatactes

Length: about 12 inches
Diet: pine nuts, other coniferous seeds, and berries
Number of Eggs: 2 to 4

Home: northern Europe and Siberia
Order: Perching birds
Family: Crows

Forests and Mountains

Birds

© DUNCAN USHER / FOTO NATURA / MINDEN PICTURES

The Eurasian nutcracker belongs to a family of very clever birds. While its cousin, the common crow, uses its intelligence to open garbage cans or unlatch gates, the Eurasian nutcracker is famous for its ability to find nuts and seeds that it buried many months earlier. In late winter, when trees are bare, the nutcracker digs through snow to uncover the treats it tucked away the previous fall.

How do these birds find their buried treasure, even beneath a blanket of fresh snow? Several other kinds of birds store food. But these less intelligent species rediscover their seeds by the trial-and-error method. The nutcracker, however, heads straight from one hidden pocket of food to the next. Experiments show that the bird uses landmarks, such as large rocks, to remember where it buried its food.

By planning ahead, nutcrackers are able to raise their families in late winter, months before other birds lay their eggs. Although snow still covers the ground, nutcrackers have plenty of hidden food to feed their chicks. Biologists estimate that a pair of nutcrackers must find at least 1,000 pockets of buried seeds to feed their brood throughout the winter.

Nutcrackers get their name from their habit of cracking the hull off pine nuts before eating them. Each bird can empty as many as 50 pinecones in one day, with each cone containing as many as 100 seeds!

Mouse Opossum
Marmosa murina

Length: 4 to 8 inches
Weight: 9 ounces
Diet: fruits and insects
Home: northern South America and Tobago

Number of Young: about 6
Order: Marsupials
Family: Mouse opossums and their relatives

 Rain forests

Mammals

© MICHAEL & PATRICIA FOGDEN / CORBIS

The cute little mouse opossum has large eyes that help it to see at night. Its big ears move in all directions to catch the slightest sound. When the mouse opossum sleeps, it folds its ears. It sleeps during the day, either in a hole in a tree or in an abandoned bird nest. When night falls, the mouse opossum becomes active, scurrying about as it looks for food.

The mouse opossum's dense fur is dark on top and white on the belly. There are black fur "eyeglasses" around the eyes. The creature's tail—scaly, hairless, and quite long—serves a very useful purpose: the tail can wrap around vines and small branches to help this little animal climb or to prevent it from falling out of trees. The mouse opossum spends its entire life in trees; it does not normally move to the ground.

Like other marsupials, mouse opossums give birth to babies that leave their mother's womb at a very early stage of development. At birth, mouse opossums are no bigger than a grain of rice! Unlike most marsupials, however, female mouse opossums do not have a pouch (marsupium). Just-born babies crawl to their mother's nipples, which are between her hind legs. There the babies remain attached, feeding on their mother's milk until they are fairly well developed. Then they spend part of the day sitting on their mother's back, using their tiny paws to hold onto the fur. If they fall off, they may start to cry; fortunately, the mother mouse opossum quickly returns to find them.

Virginia Opossum
Didelphis virginiana

Length: 15 to 20 inches without tail
Length of the Tail: 9 to 13 inches
Weight: 6 to 12 pounds
Diet: fruits and small animals

Number of Young: up to 18
Home: North, Central, and South America
Order: Marsupials
Family: Opossums

 Forests and Mountains

 Mammals

© JOE MCDONALD / CORBIS

The Virginia opossum is the only marsupial, or pouched mammal, in North America. About the size of a house cat, it has a pointed snout and a long tail that it can use to hold on to tree branches or to briefly hang upside down from a limb. The opossum rests during the day. It becomes active in the evening and wanders about until early morning looking for food. Insects and fruit are its preferred foods.

When an opossum is attacked, it defends itself by giving off a bad-smelling odor. If this does not chase off the enemy, the opossum "plays possum": it goes limp and pretends to be dead until it is left alone. Unfortunately, this defense does not work against one of the opossum's main enemies, the automobile. Many opossums are killed on highways every year.

Opossums mate two or three times a year. As many as 18 young are born at a time. But there usually are only 13 nipples in the mother's pouch to provide milk for the babies. Thus, only those babies that reach the pouch first will find nipples and be able to survive. At birth the babies are less than ½ inch long. They are hairless and blind. They remain in their mother's pouch for several weeks. Then they begin to leave the pouch for longer periods of time. They often travel on the mother's back. The babies cling to her fur with their feet or wrap their tiny tails around her tail.

Ormer

Haliotis tuberculata

Method of Reproduction: egg layer
Home: northeastern Atlantic Ocean and the Mediterranean Sea

Length: ½ to 4½ inches
Diet: algae
Order: Primitive snails
Family: Abalones

 Oceans and Shores

 Other Invertebrates

The name *ormer* comes from two Latin words: *aur*, meaning "ear," and *mer*, meaning "sea." True to its name, this little abalone shell looks like a small, dark ear that somehow got dropped into the sea. It is also called the "rough abalone" because of its uneven texture.

The ormer lives in shallow water and on wave-swept rocks, where it feeds on algae. The ormer also attaches itself to large pieces of floating kelp.

Although it is dark on the outside, the ormer's shell is colorful and shiny on the inside. This beautiful inner surface is called mother-of-pearl. It is often used to make jewelry. Like other abalone, the ormer is edible. Its meat is tasty, but even the largest ormers are only bite-sized.

Abalones such as the ormer are very primitive snails that have existed unchanged for millions of years. While modern snails tend to have high, coiled shells, the typical abalone's shell is flat, with just one broad spiral. Like most other snails, the ormer has two eyes on stalks, which extend out from under its shell. Also peeking out from its shell is a fringe of tiny tentacles. The tentacles help the ormer feel and smell its surroundings. Like all abalones the ormer has a row of holes in its shell, out of which flow water. As the ormer grows, it adds bigger holes to the row.

South African Oryx
Oryx gazella gazella

Length of the Body: 6 to 7¾ feet

Length of the Tail: 2½ to 3 feet

Diet: grasses and herbs, roots, and fruits

Height: 3¾ to 4½ feet

Weight: 400 to 500 pounds

Number of Young: 1

Home: southern Africa

Order: Even-toed hoofed mammals

Family: Bovines

 Grasslands

Mammals

© MARTIN HARVEY / PETER ARNOLD, INC.

The South African oryx is the largest and most powerful of four closely related species of oryx, all found in Africa. The South African species has bold and distinctive facial markings—three black stripes and three white ones. (Other oryx have the same pattern, but their stripes are less vivid.) This oryx also has a handsome black stripe down the middle of its back and another that runs around the sides of its belly. The oryx is famous for its long, spearlike horns. Both sexes sport horns. Also, unlike most members of the bovine family, female oryx often grow longer horns than the males.

The oryx's horns are efficient weapons. When attacking an enemy such as a lion or a hyena, the oryx lowers its head between its front legs. It then swings it horns upward to impale the predator. When fighting among themselves, oryx generally "fence" using the edges of their horns. But they do occasionally stab one another. Such bloodletting occurs most often in times of drought, when the animals must compete for overcrowded watering holes.

A large portion of the oryx's home is desert. The species survives in this harsh environment because it has an uncanny ability to find water. Sometimes locating any kind of moisture takes a heroic effort—oryx have been known to dig deep holes in dry riverbeds and to survive for days on the water they derive from roots and other buried plant matter.

Eurasian Otter
Lutra lutra

Length: 3 to 5 feet
Weight: 11 to 26 pounds
Diet: mainly fish; also shrimp, frogs, birds, and small aquatic mammals
Number of Young: 2 to 4

Home: Europe, Asia, and North Africa
Order: Carnivores
Family: Weasels and their relatives

 Fresh Water

 Mammals

© J. J. ALCALAY / PETER ARNOLD, INC.

What is the best way to get down a slippery slope or a snow-covered hill? For a Eurasian otter, the answer is easy—slide down on your belly! The Eurasian otter is very agile on land, but it is even better adapted to life in water. Its long, muscular tail and short legs with webbed feet steer and power its body. The long, streamlined body has a waterproof coat of fur that helps the Eurasian otter glide easily through water. Whiskers on the snout provide vital information about water currents and other conditions.

The Eurasian otter lives along rivers, lakes, and seashores. The creature rests during the day in its den, then comes out in the evening to hunt for food. It catches most of its food underwater and, in winter, even hunts under the thick covering of ice. The Eurasian otter's den is usually a burrow near the water, with an opening below or above the waterline as well as an opening on land. Otters also make their dens in caves and hollow logs.

Female otters give birth in a den that has been lined with grass and other soft plant matter. The babies, called whelps, are about the size of mice at birth. They are ready to leave the den when they are about two months old. At this time the whelps learn to swim, dive, and catch food. But they continue to nurse for another month or two and stay with their mother until they are one year old.

Giant Otter
Pteronura brasiliensis

Length: up to 7 feet
Weight: about 50 pounds
Number of Young: usually 2 or 3
Diet: mainly fish

Home: South America
Order: Carnivores
Family: Weasels, badgers, skunks, and otters

 Fresh Water

 Mammals

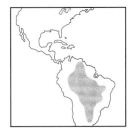

© FRANS LANTING / MINDEN PICTURES

 Endangered Animals

The giant otter lives in and along the slow-moving rivers that meander through the rain forests of eastern South America. In between fishing expeditions, the giant otter passes much of its time diving, swimming, and playing water games with its fellow otters. The giant otter joins with its brethren to hunt for fish, communicating with them via shrieks and other sounds. When it catches a fish, the otter carries it onto dry land to eat. A giant otter consumes 6 to 9 pounds of food per day.

The giant otter will dive into the water and disappear at the first sign of danger. The otter uses its webbed feet, streamlined body, and rudderlike tail to propel itself swiftly and gracefully through the water and away from danger. This swimming ability serves the otter particularly well when fleeing its main natural predators—jaguars and pumas—but does little to protect it from humans, who hunt the animal for its lustrous chocolate-brown fur. Primarily through overhunting, the giant otter now stands in danger of extinction.

The giant otter builds its den in the riverbank or under tree roots. The female gives birth to her young there and stays indoors to nurse them for several months. When it comes time for swimming lessons, the mother must often entice her young, called whelps, out of the den and into the water using a tempting mouthful of fish.

Eagle Owl
Bubo bubo

Length: 26 to 28 inches
Weight: 5 to 9 pounds
Diet: birds, small mammals, fish, and crabs
Number of Eggs: 2 to 4

Home: Europe, Asia, and northern Africa
Order: Owls
Family: Owls

Forests and Mountains

Birds

© MANFRED DEGGINGER / PETER ARNOLD, INC.

Eagle owls earn their name because their keen eyesight and fast, powerful flight resemble those of an eagle. Also like eagles, they alternate rapid wingbeats with long, straight glides and dives. The eagle owl is Europe's largest owl. The female is larger than the male, but the sexes share similar physical characteristics. Among the owl's striking features are tall ear tufts and large, glowing orange eyes. Its brown feathers are speckled with black streaks, bars, and spots.

During the day the owl sits upright and motionless in a tree hollow or rock crevice, resting with its eyes half closed. Immediately after sunset the huge bird takes flight, skimming over treetops and flying low to the ground in search of prey. Its favorite foods include small mammals, birds, and frogs. Typically the eagle owl ambushes its prey, killing it in its sleep. The owl also recklessly plunges into water after fish and crabs, and crawls into coops that house poultry.

When they are about two years old, eagle owls form lifelong pairs. The couple establishes a territory where they hunt and nest. While the female sits on the nest, the male provides food for her and their chicks. The species has greatly declined in number during the past century because it does not cope well with human disturbances. Today eagle owls are abundant only in areas where there are few people, such as steep, rocky mountains and marshy floodlands.

Little Owl
Athene noctua

Length: about 8½ inches
Weight: about 6 ounces
Diet: insects, birds, and small rodents
Number of Eggs: 3 to 6

Home: Europe, Africa, and Asia; introduced to Great Britain and New Zealand
Order: Owls
Family: Owls

 Cities, Towns, and Farms

 Birds

© STAN CRAIG / PAPILIO / CORBIS

The little owl's flattened head and piercing yellow eyes give it a fierce, angry expression. This creature is small and squat, with dark brown wings and back, speckled with white spots and bars. Despite its name the little owl is not the smallest owl in Europe. That honor belongs to the 6-inch-tall Eurasian pygmy owl.

Little owls often hunt in broad daylight. In populated areas, they perch in the open on telephone poles and fences. From such vantage points, the owl can easily dive for passing insects and scurrying mice. On occasion, little owls also eat small birds and may even pick the meat from dead animals. Little owls are especially fond of open farming country and stony hillsides, where they can readily spot their prey. When approached by a suspicious enemy, such as a human, dog, or cat, the little owl bobs and bows with alarm before flying to safety.

In Europe, little owls mate and nest from mid-April through the summer. Typically the female lays her eggs in a tree hole or in a crevice in a rock or building. Occasionally a mated pair will move into the abandoned burrow of a squirrel or other rodent. Once she lays her eggs, the female stays in the nest for about a month, rarely leaving. During this time the male brings her food. He also feeds the chicks when they hatch. The mother joins her mate in hunting and feeding the young a few days later.

Yellow-Billed Oxpecker
Buphagus africanus

Length: 9 inches
Diet: ticks and flies
Number of Eggs: 2 to 5

Home: central Africa
Order: Perching birds
Family: Starlings

Grasslands

Birds

© YANN ARTHUS-BERTRAND / CORBIS

A flock of yellow-billed oxpeckers travel across the African plains in an unusual way: riding on the backs of such animals as wild buffalo and zebra. But this is no free ride—the oxpeckers are on tick patrol. With their strong, sharp bills, these birds can pull ticks out of the toughest animal hide. The nimble oxpecker will even run up to an animal's head to clean ticks from the ears and nose. This bird also catches pesky flies buzzing around an ox's face and body. The oxpecker's grooming helps to keep its host healthy and comfortable. At the same time, the insects provide the oxpecker with a nutritious, high-protein diet.

In addition to a heavy bill for plucking ticks, nature has given the oxpecker strong feet and long, sharp claws for clinging to its mount. From its safe perch on a buffalo's head or a zebra's rump, the oxpecker has a good view of the surrounding grasslands. The bird is a dependable lookout and will call out loudly if wild dogs or other predators approach. Its cry will send an entire herd of wild oxen thundering across the savanna.

Despite its exotic appearance and lifestyle, the yellow-billed oxpecker is a close relative of the common starling. This family of birds shares the oxpecker's love of insects, its sturdy bill and legs, and its dark, somewhat dull plumage. In the oxpecker's case, both male and female look alike. Like all starlings, oxpeckers are songbirds whose voices sound much like noisy whistles.

Gray Parrot
Psittacus erithacus

Length: 13 inches
Diet: seeds, fruits, nuts, and berries
Number of Eggs: 2 to 4

Home: equatorial Africa
Order: Parrots
Family: True parrots

 Forests and Mountains

 Birds

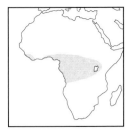

© JANE BURTON / BRUCE COLEMAN INC.

For centuries the gray parrot has been a popular household pet—even among royalty. England's King Henry VIII, who reigned during the 1500s, had a pet gray parrot. A gray parrot was the beloved companion of a duke in the court of England's King Charles II during the 1600s. In fact, the oldest known stuffed bird is a gray parrot. The bird even appears in fiction: perhaps the most famous one belonged to Long John Silver, a character in *Treasure Island* by Robert Louis Stevenson.

In the wild, gray parrots live in flocks that may number several hundred birds. At night they sleep while roosting on high tree branches near the edge of lowland forests and mangrove swamps. At sunrise, they fly to their feeding grounds. The birds eat mainly oil-palm nuts and other foods found in treetops. For a treat, however, they sometimes raid farmers' cornfields, causing quite a bit of damage. They return to their roosts at sunset.

After mating, the female gray parrot lays two to four white eggs in the hole of a tree, high above the ground. She incubates the eggs until they hatch—in about four weeks. The female feeds the babies during their first week of life, after which the male begins to help out. Both parents feed their young by regurgitating partly digested food. The young parrots grow fast and are ready to leave the nest when they are about 10 weeks old.

Turquoise Parrot
Neophema pulchella

Length: about 8 inches
Weight: about 1⅓ ounces
Diet: seeds and leaves
Number of Eggs: 4 or 5

Home: southeastern Australia
Order: Parrots
Family: Parrots

 Forests and Mountains

 Birds

© HANS REINHARD / BRUCE COLEMAN INC.

Unlike most parrots, the turquoise species is quiet and gentle. While their cousins screech and holler in large, noisy flocks, turquoise parrots live singly, in pairs, or in small, peaceful groups. In the heat of the day, these birds sit quietly in shady trees and shrubs. They wait patiently for the cooler hours, when they hop to the ground and pace back and forth in search of seeds. Instead of screeching and squawking, this parrot twitters quietly as it feeds. Even its mating call is demure, little more than a soft whistle.

Both sexes are beautifully colored with a blue face and green body. However, the male is much brighter and can be recognized by a red band on the top of each wing. Young turquoise parrots are duller than their parents.

Turquoise parrots court and mate between August and December. The female constructs a nest in the hollow of a stump, tree, or fence post. Once she lays her eggs, the female diligently incubates them. The chicks learn to fly when they are about four weeks old.

Although they are quiet, these rare parrots are far from shy. While feeding, they allow humans to pass nearby. Sometimes they even follow farm trucks, waiting to feed on spilled grain. Their natural diet includes the seeds of chickweed, barley grass, and Australia's native wallaby grass.

Red-Legged Partridge
Alectoris rufa

Number of Eggs: usually 10 to 16

Diet: mainly seeds, berries, and other plant matter; also insects

Length: 13 inches
Home: Western Europe
Order: Game birds
Family: Pheasants and quails

 Grasslands

 Birds

Although the red-legged partridge can fly, this stout-bodied bird spends most of its time on the ground. The partridge loves to hide in vegetation, where it can eat and live in safety. The red-legged partridge settles in marshes, fields, farmland, or on hillsides. The brownish colors of its feathers allow the partridge to blend into all of these surroundings with ease.

The partridge has a thick red bill and, as you might expect, a set of matching red legs. These strong legs are armed with nails that are specially designed for scratching the ground for food. The red-legged partridge likes to eat seeds, berries, roots, and other plant matter, but it will also occasionally eat ants and other insects. The partridge prefers to feed in the early morning and in the evening.

In the spring the female partridge, called a hen, uses her sharp claws to scratch out a simple hollow to make her nest. She covers the floor of the nest with grass and dead leaves. The hen incubates her eggs for about 24 days while the male, called a cock, stands guard over the nest. The hen and the cock rear their chicks together. The chicks mature quickly and can fly when they are just a few weeks old. However, the chicks stay with their parents until the next breeding season. Families of partridges do not migrate south in the winter. Instead, they spend the colder months together with other families in flocks, called coveys.

Collared Peccary
Tayassu tajacu

Length: 2½ to 3½ feet
Weight: up to 68 pounds
Diet: fruits, acorns, nuts, roots, grasses, and small animals
Number of Young: 2 to 6

Home: North, Central, and South America
Order: Even-toed hoofed mammals
Family: Peccaries

Rain forests

Mammals

© D. ROBERT & LORRI FRANZ / CORBIS

The Tupi Indians of Brazil have a word for "the animal that makes many paths through the woods." That word is "peccary." The collared peccary lives in South America, where it is a forest animal. In the woods and jungles of Brazil, families of collared peccaries run, single file, down narrow paths of their own making. However, the collared peccary has learned to live in many different habitats. It ranges as far north as Arizona and Texas, where it can be found in brushy deserts and rocky canyons.

In the South American rain forest, peccaries enjoy year-round warmth. But in North America, they must survive major changes in temperature. During the summer, they avoid the strong desert sun by grazing in the early morning and at twilight. Midday is a time for sleeping in the shade of a cave or a bush. But in winter, North American peccaries must seek warmth. They are active during the day and sleep cuddled together at night. The black tips of the peccary's bristles help absorb the sun's heat during the winter. They break off during the summer, giving the peccary a lighter, cooler coat.

The collared peccary, with a distinctive white ring around its shoulders, is one of three species in its family. Peccaries give birth throughout the year, usually to twins. The young often stay with their parents for their entire lives. When newborn arrive, older sisters help care for them and sometimes even nurse them.